DIAL 9
TO GET OUT!

DIAL 9 TO GET OUT!

Commentaries on Business Life
as heard on Public Radio's *Marketplace*

DAVID GRAULICH

Berrett-Koehler Publishers
San Francisco

Berrett-Koehler Publishers, Inc.
155 Montgomery St.
San Francisco, CA 94104-4109
Tel: 415-288-0260   Fax: 415-362-2512

HF
5007
.G72
1994

ORDERING INFORMATION
Individual sales. Berrett-Koehler publications are available through bookstores. They can also be ordered direct from Berrett-Koehler at the address above.

Quantity sales. Berrett-Koehler publications are available on quantity purchases by corporations, associations, and others. For details, contact the "Special Sales Department" at the Berrett-Koehler address above.

Orders for college textbook/course adoption use. Please contact Berrett-Koehler Publishers at the address above.

Orders by U.S. trade bookstores and wholesalers. Please contact Publishers Group West, 4065 Hollis St., Box 8843, Emeryville, CA 94662; tel. 510-658-3453; 1-800-788-3123.

Printed in the United States of America

Printed on acid-free and recycled paper that meets the strictest state and U.S. guidelines for recycled paper (50 percent recycled waste, including 10 percent postconsumer waste).

Library of Congress Cataloging-in-Publication Data
Graulich, David J.
    Dial 9 to get out! / David Graulich. -- 1st ed.
       p. cm.
    ISBN 1-881052-50-8
    1. Business--Anecdotes. 2. Business--Humor. 3. Work--Anecdotes.
4. Work--Humor. I. Title.
HF5007.G72 1994
650'.0207--dc20
                                                  94-3958
                                                CIP

First Edition
  99 98 97 96 95 94 93   10 9 8 7 6 5 4 3 2 1

TO REBECCA

CONTENTS

PREFACE

When I began these radio commentaries for *Marketplace* back in 1989, I thought I would have enough material for perhaps four or five pieces before exhausting my ideas and concluding my brief career in broadcasting. I did not realize that in choosing the whimsical and eccentric aspects of business life as my subject area, I had struck a mother lode.

Soon I was getting ideas from everywhere. A friend at a poker game told me about the "complaint jar" in his office, which became "The Fine Art of Complaining." A *Marketplace* listener who worked at a snack food factory recounted how she had to assemble a flawless bag of immaculate potato chips for the company president's lunch, which provided material for "When the Big Boss Comes to Visit." A neighbor who looked a bit tired told me why he was working so hard, which ended up as "Two-Weeks' Notice." The anecdotes from another *Marketplace* listener who had just attended an exhausting computer convention in Las Vegas led to "Surviving a Trade Show" and "Breaking Through the Ad Clutter."

Indeed, it seems that anyone who has ever held a job has some bizarre experience, incredible revelation, or ironic episode that he or she is eager to retell. Although many of these commentaries are derived from my own experiences in corporate life, I find I have also become a sounding board and chronicler for other people who approach with a wicked grin and say, "You know, here's something you ought to use on *Marketplace*. You won't believe this! When I worked at XYZ Corporation, we had this crazy policy, etc., etc."

Dero Saunders, who retired a few years ago as a senior editor of *Forbes*, once told me that there were three great themes in human life—love, war, and work—and that while artists, musicians, and writers had devoted immense energies to the first two, they had left the third relatively untouched. I have often thought of Dero's remark while writing these commentaries. When it comes to life in the business world, there are a million stories out there, and several million highly motivated storytellers. The canvas is vast. All a creative person really has to do to find great material is listen.

When people tell me their stories, one phrase comes up a lot: "This place is driving me nuts. Someday I'm going to get out of here!" I have heard this from chief executives, middle managers, and entry-level workers—the sentiment transcends rank, title, and salary level. I have heard it from people who are unhappy at work, which is not surprising, but also from people who really enjoy their jobs, who like the companies they work for, who are well compensated, and who get along rather nicely with their coworkers. Everyone, it seems, wants to be seen as a lone figure of sanity and sensibility in the midst of general corporate craziness; that is, someone who is *just this close* to bailing out of the place for good.

I am not sure what causes this phenomenon. Nevertheless, the title of this collection, *Dial 9 to Get Out!*, recognizes those huddled business masses who insist that they are yearning to "get out" (to points unknown) and who will proclaim their yearnings to a stranger at the slightest provocation. The desire to "get out" is as universal as a dial tone and as inevitable as the "9" that an office worker needs for an outside telephone line.

It is true that the title contains an outdated word: one does not *dial* a phone anymore, but *punches*, *touches*, *strikes*, or *enters*. However, I'm fond of this verbal anachronism and find it oddly appropriate. Most business offices have telephone equipment that hardly anyone knows how to use, beyond picking up a phone when it rings. A guaranteed way to confuse a self-assured executive is to ask that your call be transferred to another extension or that the speakerphone be activated. "Um, I don't know how to do that. Could you call back?" the executive will say. *Dial 9 to Get Out!* proudly salutes these high-tech phone systems and their low-tech users.

In choosing the best forty one commentaries from the past four years for this collection, I have included several where a name or reference has been overtaken by the passage of time. While sharp-eyed readers will detect these, I hope the overall value of the material does not suffer as a result. I have also included a few commentaries in which I depart from my main subject and talk about some pet peeve, such as intrusive ads in doctors' waiting rooms, but primarily the focus is on life in the business world.

I am indebted to quite a few people. Penny Dennis, the *Marketplace* producer for most of these commentaries, has been a steady source of encouragement and wise counsel. Monty Carlos and the engineering staff at KQED-FM in San Francisco worked diligently so that the tapings were of high technical quality, and also made the recording sessions a lot of fun. Herb Stansbury, author, cartoonist, and bank chairman, suggested the concept for this book and has been a terrific coach and friend.

Steven Piersanti and the entire team at Berrett-Koehler Publishers have been champions of my work and first-class creative partners. My parents, brother, and sister exhibited a splendid sense of humor by raising me. Buddy, my Bouvier des Flandres dog and head of strategic planning for Maxfield Public Relations, has displayed the best qualities of his breed while avoiding the worst qualities of ours. Finally, my wife, Rebecca, has been a sharp, talented, and patient editor for these commentaries, as well as a source of good ideas drawn from her own business career.

David Graulich
San Bruno, California
February 1994

THE WONDERFUL WORLD OF WORK

ELEVATOR BUDDY

*A*nyone who works in a large office building has a special kind of friend known as an elevator buddy. An elevator buddy is someone employed in the same building as you, but not in the same office or the same company. You just see him riding up and down in the elevator.

You greet each other in the morning and say goodbye at the end of the workday. You find out where he lives, what company he works for, and how long his commute is. Each conversation only lasts for seconds, but multiply those snippets over years and a saga unfolds.

It may not seem like much of a friendship, but when you think about it, your elevator buddy knows most of the major events in your life. He sees you with suitcases and flight bags and knows you're leaving for a long trip. He compliments your tan when you've returned from vacation. When you show up bleary-eyed and bewildered, he finds out that you've been up all night with a new baby.

If you meet on Friday evening, you always say to each other, "Have a nice weekend," and on Monday mornings you always ask, "Did you have a nice weekend?"

You only talk with your elevator buddy on the elevator. The rules are that once the elevator hits the lobby and the doors open, you quickly end the conversation and go your separate ways. It would be rude and ridiculous to follow your elevator buddy out the building and down the street, still talking.

Sometimes weeks go by and you don't see your elevator buddy. You wonder if he's changed jobs and regret not having had the chance to wish him good luck. Then you'll see him again on the elevator some dark, rainy Monday morning and feel pleased. Or you may find out months later that his company laid people off or relocated its office to the other side of the country, and you'll realize that your elevator buddy is gone.

So, for all of those elevator buddies who have moved on and whom we'll never see again, here's a simple thanks—thanks for your friendship, for your companionship and good cheer, and for riding with us through life's ups and downs.

BUSINESS SWEARING

I don't know if you can measure this, but it seems like there's been an enormous increase in the amount of swearing, cursing, and off-color language in the business world. Sit in any meeting of white-collar workers and before long the conversation is laced with most of the known curse words in the English language, as well as a few colorful obscenities imported from overseas. The more high-paid and powerful the people are, the more likely they are to talk dirty.

In most professions, it used to be that blue language was bad form. The breakthrough may have been the release of the Nixon White House tapes in 1974, when expletives— deleted or otherwise—filled the Oval Office. Since then, the obscenity utilization index, if there is such a thing, has gone through the roof.

Michael Korda, the writer and publisher, once observed a certain structure to business cursing. It starts when the senior-most executive at a meeting utters a mild profanity for shock effect. The junior executives, wanting to prove that they're staunch members of the team, start swearing a little more strongly. Women at the meeting, to show that they're not intimidated by this locker-room atmosphere, escalate things with earthy language of their own. Before long, profanities are zinging all over the place until the conference room sounds like a convention of longshoremen.

My problem with this is not one of morality, but of quality. The truth is that most of us white-collar types are pretty inept when it comes to creative swearing. We can't get the rhythm or the phrasing quite right. Basically, we sound like wimps when we curse.

It gets really strange when a corporate big shot attempts to swear in the style of jive street talk, as if this high-powered–MBA–Yale Law School–Brooks Brothers–squash-playing investment banker is really a supercool bad dude straight out of a rap music video. The result isn't profane, it's just plain silly.

There are times, of course, when a good old-fashioned Anglo-Saxon phrase is exactly right to express an idea or emotion. But when you hear someone in business constantly resorting to four-letter words, you've got to wonder if it's just a substitute for having to think.

THE LUNCHROOM

---

n the movies, business lunches take place in elegant restaurants filled with fine china and fancy food. In real life, however, most business lunches get eaten in the company lunchroom, or canteen. This is usually a small room with linoleum tile and some vending machines; a coffeemaker, microwave, and refrigerator; a few tables and chairs of the type favored by hospitals and junior high schools; and a bulletin board.

No matter what business your company is in, where it is located, or its financial condition, there are certain fundamental truths about the employee lunchroom.

One is that the lunchroom always doubles as a storage place for all those things from around the office that don't fit anywhere else. So, you're likely to eat your lunch while sitting next to a broken IBM Selectric typewriter and a year's supply of used Velobinders.

Another is that there is always an angry handwritten note on the refrigerator door that says: "Someone ate my baloney and cheddar cheese sandwich and peach yogurt last Tuesday. They were on the bottom shelf in a brown bag clearly marked Betty. Whoever did this is a jerk. Signed, Betty." There will also be a stern typewritten note from the office administrator, full of capital letters and underlined words, warning that the refrigerator will be cleaned out every Friday at five o'clock and anything left will be THROWN OUT, NO EXCEPTIONS.

On the bulletin board, someone is always selling a blue 1971 VW bus, good condition. Someone else who lives 140 miles from the office is looking for a roommate, and the nearest amusement park is offering discount tickets for a special employee day at the park. There will also be elaborate instructions on the coffeemaker for how to clean it out and make new coffee—instructions that will be ignored by everyone, resulting in a tiny amount of old coffee perpetually washing around in the bottom of the pot.

Now, the company lunchroom may not win any dining awards, but it does serve a valuable purpose. With so many people changing jobs and moving around the country, it's comforting to know that there's one place where you can feel surrounded by the familiar and constant. And, if you are new at the job and know anything about that missing baloney sandwich—tell Betty.

CARLESS COWORKERS

Is somebody in your office acting a bit strange this week? Don't take it personally. It might be that he or she has become a carless coworker.

Carless coworkers are people who need automobiles to get to work, but whose car is in the shop for repairs. This may not seem like a big deal if you live and work in a city, but if your job is in a suburban office complex off an interstate highway, carlessness is a very bad thing.

Carless coworkers show clear signs of distress. They spend hours studying bus and train schedules, trying to figure out the difference between A.M. and P.M. departures, wondering whether the 5:02 Express stops at their stop, and repeatedly counting coins to make sure they have the necessary exact change. Public transit is an alien concept to these people.

Carlessness converts even the most hard-driving business executive into a pedestrian wimp. How can you stay on the corporate fast track, when you don't even have a set of wheels?

A suddenly carless coworker will ask you leading questions, such as, "Say, by any chance do you go down Route 280 on your way home from work, and are you planning to leave between 5:45 and 6 o'clock?" Or they badger the message center to see if the repair shop has called yet with an estimate, and then stagger around the office looking anguished when they hear how much it will cost to fix their car. Or they suddenly volunteer to take long business trips out of town, where they don't have to worry about commuting to the office.

So don't be surprised when a coworker who has never showed any interest in socializing before—someone who has barely acknowledged your existence—shows up at your desk one morning, smiles, and asks, "Would you like to go out for lunch today? You wanna drive?"

THE FINE ART
OF COMPLAINING

A basic right of the American workplace is the right to complain about your job. No matter where your office is, what you get paid, or who signs your check, there's one thing for sure—you have the right to complain about what you do for a living.

A friend works for the marketing department of a publishing company. So much time was being taken up with complaining that the department decided to create a "complaint jar." Whenever anyone starts complaining, he or she must toss a quarter in the complaint jar. At the end of the month, the complaint jar takes the whole department out to lunch. During particularly stressed-out times, some people whip out a ten-dollar bill when they get to work in the morning and stuff it right into the complaint jar, so they'll be set for a whole day of heavy-duty complaining. My friend predicts that eventually the company will take complaint jar deductions directly from his paychecks, as an employee benefit.

Job complaints take many forms. There's low-tech complaining, such as the graffiti scribbled in company restrooms. There's high-tech complaining, in which you transmit unhappy little messages through E-mail to vast numbers of sympathizers. There's everyday run-of-the-mill whining, griping, and grumbling, which no one, including the complainer and the complainee, takes very seriously. There's full-blown memo-length complaining, which, according to the management experts, is not really complaining at all but "utilization of communication channels to provide meaningful feedback."

One classic complaint goes to the tune of, "Those Were the Days, My Friend." It is often found at high-tech companies in Silicon Valley that are just beyond the start-up stage. In the early days, people will tell you, the bonus checks were bigger, the Christmas parties more lavish, and the spirit was really something to see. Now, of course, everything has changed for the worse. Nothing is as good as it *used* to be.

If you take this talk at face value, it can drive you crazy—you'll go through your whole career thinking that you've *just* missed the boat at every new company you join. So, the best response is to nod your head, wear an understanding expression, and remind the complainers to put, oh, about five bucks in the complaint jar.

LARKS AND OWLS

There's a form of discrimination in Corporate America that most people don't know about. That's the discrimination that morning people, also known as larks, practice against evening people, also known as owls.

Larks are at their chipper best in the earliest hours of the day. They are the ones whistling on the platform as they wait for the commuter train and shouting out cheerful "Good Mornings" as they stride energetically to their desks. Owls, on the other hand, face the mornings with fear and loathing, muttering dark curses as they stir their coffee. But owls come alive and get productive as the late afternoon turns into the early evening, just when the larks are drooping and fluttering back to their nests.

The problem is that the business world is basically run by the larks. They make their way of life seem so virtuous. They call 7 A.M. breakfast meetings to show off their perkiness. They tell customers, "I'll get to it first thing in the morning," as if that is something wonderful. When owls say, "I'll get to it at the end of the day," they sound like laggards. Maybe it's a leftover from when America was a farming society, and "early to bed, early to rise" was the rule.

Well, most of us don't live on the farm anymore, and as a member of the oppressed group, I think it's time to stop the anti-owl bias. Owls deserve a little respect. For example, Tom Watson, Sr., the founder of IBM, was an owl. According to the memoirs recently written by his son, Watson didn't really get going until 5 P.M., when he'd be overflowing with ideas and projects. And biologists say that extroverts are usually owls, while introverts tend to be larks.

So if you are a boss who is a lark, please be more sensitive to the needs of your owl workers. Be aware of the dread with which they struggle in the dawn's early light. From an owl's point of view, there's only one thing tougher than having to work for a lark—and that's being married to one.

GRATITUDE INFLATION

There's a writing assignment that makes even professional writers flinch. It's only two paragraphs long, requires no research, and the reader usually discards it within seconds.

The little demon that I'm describing is the business thank you note. You feel obliged to write one after somebody has granted you a small favor, like letting you use a conference room or taking you to lunch. You then wrap yourself into knots trying to write something that doesn't sound maudlin or mechanical, that walks the line between trite and tortured, that strikes a balance between warmth and wimpiness.

Writing a decent business thank you note was always tough, but in recent years it has become almost impossible due to what may be called gratitude inflation. This started with George Bush and his highly publicized, handwritten thank you notes to prime ministers and peons alike. Now marketing gurus and career counselors are loudly proclaiming thank you notes as a surefire means of self-promotion and networking. Send thank you notes—dozens and dozens of thank you notes—and you're *guaranteed* to get ahead, say these so-called experts.

The result is that the sincerity level of the typical business thank you note has shrunken to microscopic dimensions. Pass the sugar to somebody you don't know at a business luncheon and you will get a thank you note dripping in simulated sentiment. Worse yet, the sender, whose name you have already forgotten, vows to stay in touch with you faithfully for decades to come. The trend is that the more trivial the favor you extend, the more extravagant—and bogus—the thank you note you'll receive.

Like monetary inflation, gratitude inflation destroys people's faith in their means of exchange. It's time we take the air out of this hot air bubble of counterfeit thankfulness. You can start by declaring your office a phony-thank-you free zone: overwrought expressions of thanks will neither be extended nor accepted. This may seem harsh, but we must do something before what used to be called "the still small voice of gratitude" is drowned in a sea of artificial appreciation.

THINKING IN THE SHOWER

sk people where they do their best thinking and one answer comes up time and again: the shower. There must be something about the heat and steam, or maybe it's getting out of those inhibiting work clothes. Many people insist that the shower is where they come up with creative concepts, inspired strategies, and breakthrough ideas.

The problem is that by the time you dry off, get dressed, and commute to work, you forget most everything. There's a lack of the productivity tools that surround you while you are sitting at your desk, high and dry and suffering from brain-lock. So here are suggestions for devices that will help people when they are scrubbing, lathering, rinsing, and doing their best thinking.

It would be great to have a voice-activated dictaphone embedded in the shower stall that could record you shouting out your great ideas, while automatically screening out the sound of running water. A side benefit of this gadget is that it would also capture you performing "Man of La Mancha" or other singing-in-the-shower masterpieces.

Of course, it would also be great to have a personal computer in the shower so you could transmit instant E-mail messages. The screen could be made from the same material used for bathroom shaving mirrors that don't fog over. Instead of a keyboard, the mouse could double as a bar of soap. And there should be towels decorated in graph-paper patterns so you can jot down quick charts.

Furthermore, the corporate workday should allow for at least one on-site shower break, after which all the senior executives would convene in a conference room—draped modestly in towels, of course—to act upon their great ideas.

In today's tough global economy America needs every advantage it can get. The waste of shower intellect is a national disaster. We can no longer afford to let some of our most creative and brilliant thinking simply go down the drain.

MY BUSINESS
ROCK 'N' ROLL COUNTDOWN

There is a book out called *The Heart of Rock & Soul,* which lists the 1,001 greatest rock and soul singles ever recorded. Certain topics show up a lot in this list, like boys meeting girls, surfboards, fast cars, broken hearts, and groovy kinds of love. But one subject that doesn't show up very much in this list is business. So I've made a list of the four greatest rock 'n' roll songs of all time that have a business theme. Here goes:

In the Number Four position—"Taking Care of Business" by Bachman-Turner Overdrive, 1974. Combines a steady dance beat with a wry commentary on doing hardly anything all day—and working overtime at it. Also one of the great fraternity party tunes of this century.

Jumping into the Number Three position is—"Five O'Clock World" by the Vogues, 1973. Wonderful gritty lyrics of a man laboring at his job and battling the long urban commute home. An unforgettable yodel between verses is another great feature of this tune.

Holding down the Number Two spot is—"Get a Job" by The Silhouettes, 1958. The lyrics tell about a guy getting out of bed, reading the paper through and through in search of a job while getting harassed by his girlfriend. This tells you more about unemployment than anything you'll ever read from the Bureau of Labor Statistics. Also rates as the greatest doo-wop song ever, which gave birth to the phrase "Sha-Na-Na."

And finally, the Number One rock 'n' roll song about business of all time: "Money," first recorded by Barrett Strong in 1960, later recorded by many other groups, including the Beatles. The lyrics—"Money, money, that's what I want"—anticipated the yuppie revolution by more than twenty years, and the song was also one of the first hits written by Motown's Berry Gordy. These twin peaks of history earn it the Number One position on our list.

So there you have it—the four greatest business rock 'n' roll songs of all time. No, business will never replace fast cars and pretty women as favorite subjects for rock music. But at least now the tunes that *do* sing about business can get a little r-e-s-p-e-c-t.

THE BOSS: CARE AND FEEDING OF

WHEN THE BIG BOSS
COMES TO VISIT

E very so often there's a photograph in the newspaper that gives Americans a good laugh. It
shows England's Prince Charles arriving at some
distant outpost of the British Empire, where he's being
greeted by a tribal leader in full native dress and led off
to attend a ritual dance or pig roast.

Well, we should remember that this little scene, or
something very much like it, is repeated every week in
America. That's when the CEO of a big company decides
to leave headquarters in New York, Chicago, or Los Angeles to visit one of the company's plants in some far-off
location like Kenly, North Carolina; Jackson, Mississippi;
or Gilroy, California.

Now, a plant visit isn't a bad idea. A CEO might even
learn something about how his company makes its products. But most of the time the CEO's visit is as carefully
choreographed as a visit by Prince Charles. From the
moment his limo pulls up in front of the plant to the time

he is whisked away to the closest thing the area has to a four-star hotel, his movements and conversations are minutely scheduled.

Sometimes the boss will have a symbolic lunch with a selected group of employees, which results in a painfully stilted conversation. And there's always a goofy moment when the CEO puts on a hairnet and walks down the assembly line, while a photographer for the company magazine records the scene for posterity.

Meanwhile, the plant is thrown into chaos and the plant manager suffers through his worst day of the year. One misstep could blow his career. He's probably had his maintenance budget cut back and can't have the lawns mowed or the floors swept as frequently. But everything has to be spruced up for the CEO's visit, with fresh flowers put in the reception area and everybody warned to be on best behavior. All of a sudden every office *must* have a new trash can and the banisters on the stairway have to be immaculately painted, lest the CEO's eye be offended. Everyone in the plant is shouting at one another in a state of panic, to be replaced by saccharine sweetness once the honored guest arrives.

Imagine the sigh of relief that sweeps through the plant when the CEO's limo finally rolls away into the sunset. Come to think of it, I wonder if Prince Charles's departure evokes the same emotion in those tribal chieftains.

THE BOSS'S VACATION

With the peak of summer approaching, millions of American workers are about to encounter the most stressful and aggravating time of the year: their boss is going on vacation.

Surviving your boss's vacation takes a great deal of strength and endurance. For days leading up to the vacation, your boss will be issuing a blizzard of warning memos, demanding that all sorts of things be done before he or she goes off to points remote.

Meanwhile, great piles of work start migrating from your boss's desk onto *yours*, accompanied by flocks of Post-It™ notes urgently asking you to handle this or that mess.

Once the boss leaves, an uneasy quiet settles over the office, during which you and your colleagues try to get things done exactly as the boss would want them. The calm is broken by the phone call of you-know-who from Martha's Vineyard, Malibu, Mackinaw Island, or Maui.

The call will probably arrive two minutes after you leave your desk to make some photocopies. Should you actually take the call, you will be required to make reassurances that the business, by some miracle, has managed to survive during the boss's absence—although naturally things would be *much* better if the boss was actually there.

Sooner or later the boss returns to the office—usually extra early in the morning, as if to send a clear signal that "fun time" is over. Everyone makes the obligatory compliments about the boss's tan and rejuvenated appearance. Then it's time to review everything that happened during the boss's vacation, find out everything you did wrong, and present whatever didn't get done because "we decided it was better to wait until you got back." And a new wave of urgent memos surges out of the boss's office and right toward your in-box, like a heat-seeking missile, as the boss struggles heroically to get caught up.

If you *are* a boss, you may not have realized the high stress that your vacation creates. You didn't notice the subtle clues—like the fact that everyone who works for you simultaneously announces that he or she needs a vacation after you come back from your vacation. Listen to these people with sympathy. They've come to realize that the only thing worse than having you, the boss, hanging around the office is the prospect of *not* having you, the boss, hanging around the office.

THE MOST POWERFUL PEOPLE
IN CORPORATE AMERICA*

I've been looking through a business magazine that has photos and capsule biographies of the one thousand most powerful people in Corporate America. It's fascinating to read this list. But even more fascinating are the questions left unanswered about these big shots and their businesses.

For example, why does Robert Baker, head of a company called Vermont American, have headquarters in Louisville, Kentucky? What was the reason for "the unexpected slump in deaths" that made profits go down at Service Corp., a franchiser of funeral homes? Why does Peter Lewis of Progressive, an insurance company, sign his annual report "Joy, Love, and Peace"?

Why are there so many companies I've never heard of that start with the letter N—can you honestly say that you recognize Newell, NCH, Nacco, Nerco, or Nipsco?

* Broadcast on January 23, 1990.

Does David *A.* Jones, the top man at Humana, ever get advice from David *C.* Jones, the boss of National Education Corp., or from David *R.* Jones, who runs the show for Atlanta Gas Light? For that matter, Neiman Marcus and General Cinema Corp. both have CEOs named Richard A. Smith. Do they ever go shopping and to the movies together? Or are they the same person?

Why is Leon Levine of Family Dollar Stores the only CEO whose favorite sport is bowling? How did Roy Park of Park Communications start his hobby, watching and raising peacocks? How did the CEO of Beneficial start his hobby of four-in-hand carriage racing? By the way, what *is* four-in-hand carriage racing?

And, finally, why do I so much admire Winston R. Wallin, CEO of Medtronic? Actually, this is the only question I can answer. I admire Mr. Wallin because among these superstars who spend their weekends flying planes, running marathons, or playing cutthroat tennis, Mr. Wallin says that his favorite spare-time activity is— "doing absolutely nothing."

PERKS

There is a new survey out of perks, the ways corporations give special compensation to their top executives. Most of the perks are pretty traditional, such as country club memberships, company cars, and first-class air travel.

But some of the perks listed in the survey seem a little strange. Although 19 percent of the companies offer a health club membership, a full 32 percent give executives a reserved parking spot. Wouldn't it make more sense to have less reserved parking so that executives can get a brisk walk to and from their cars every day?

And while 55 percent of the big shots receive a luncheon club membership as a perk, only 30 percent get an on-site executive dining room, which suggests that food tastes better as you get further away from your office.

All these perks are fine, but I can think of two other very important ones not mentioned in the survey:

Perk No. 1 — The company reimburses you for money given to office gift collections. You know, when the nice person comes around and asks for two dollars so the department can buy a baby gift for the receptionist on the other side of the building who is having her fifth kid? The receptionist you've spoken with, oh, maybe three times in the last ten years? With this perk, the company would reimburse any and all of these donations, protecting both your reputation for friendliness and your wallet.

Perk No. 2 —You are exempt from having to wear one of those dumb T-shirts that say something inspirational about your company or which make some double-entendre put-down of your main competitor. These T-shirts are all the rage these days at sales conferences, motivational workshops, and other company gatherings, where the idea is that everybody spontaneously pulls the T-shirt over his business suit, chants the slogan, and sits grinning at one another. Give me a really valuable perk like that—and I'd even be willing to skip the executive dining room.

OUR CORPORATE FAMILY

There is one place left in America where the old-fashioned nuclear family, 1950s style, still exists. That's in the pages of the typical in-house magazine that corporations publish for their employees.

First, there's Dad, the company president, who smiles warmly from the special page up front, reserved just for him. Dad's comments are usually vaguely optimistic and incredibly dull. Like most Dads, the company president is a nice fellow, a bit remote, not a very good communicator, but always upbeat and positive. Like Ozzie Nelson on the *Ozzie and Harriet* show, no one is quite sure what the president does every day, but he is always lingering somewhere nearby with a smile and a kind word.

Mom is not usually shown in these magazines, but there's no mistaking her presence. All those articles that nag, warn, or admonish us to be better workers and better people: Stop smoking—Save electricity—Support the United Way—Get in shape—Don't waste office supplies.

There are also "mommy" articles with inspiring themes about our wonderful coworkers: the fellow on the loading dock who has forty-three adopted children, the secretary who won a gold medal for her apple pie recipe, the truck driver who is a part-time country music singer.

The extended family is also represented. There's Grandfather, the company's beloved founder, pictured in his flowing white beard and top hat. Grandfather's wise words are still remembered and closely followed. In fact, Dad often quotes Grandfather on his special page.

Then, there are photographs of our aunts and uncles and cousins who work in exotic locations around the globe. Here's Uncle Fred, who used to be down the hall in accounts payable, standing next to a Zulu tribesman! Here's our new machine tool plant next to the Pyramids! There's Cousin Willie—what a goofy little kid he was— signing a big contract in Venezuela!

In the real world, a lot of corporate families are being broken up by takeovers, mergers, and leveraged buyouts. So it's nice to know that in the peaceful little world of company magazines, life is still *Leave It to Beaver, My Three Sons,* and *Father Knows Best* rolled into one.

SYMBOLIC ACTIONS

These are tough times in Corporate America and that translates into good times for—symbolic actions. These are actions that top executives take primarily to show how serious, tough-minded, and take-charge they are, and to "send a message" to employees.

Corporations always do symbolic things, like putting catchy slogans on their postal meter stamps or decorating the commuter vanpools with the company's colors. But bad profits seem to bring out the best in symbolic activists.

For example, the former head of purchasing at General Motors wanted to overhaul how GM did business with suppliers. He told his staff to move their wristwatches from the left wrist to the right wrist. The symbolism? Times have changed. Now, that was pretty good symbolism. But with the continuing turmoil and layoffs at the big automaker, this purchasing executive has left the company. The next symbolic action might be to remove the wristwatches altogether.

On a more upbeat note, there's the symbolic action taken by a branch manager at U.S. Bancorp in Portland, Oregon. He was angered by the fees charged by a lawn-care service to cut the branch's grass. So he fired the service and cut the grass himself each weekend with his own mower. This might go beyond mere symbolism and become a new banking product: get your home mortgage at U.S. Bancorp and, for a small additional fee, the branch manager will show up on Saturdays to mow your loan, uh, lawn.

Then there's the symbolic action taken by Marvin Mann, chairman of Lexmark, a company that makes printers and typewriters and was spun off recently from IBM. Mr. Mann wants Lexmark employees to think more on their own and not rely on a bureaucracy, like they did at IBM, so his symbolic action was to abolish the suggestion box.

That's right, he banned the very item so beloved by management theorists—the humble suggestion box. Mr. Mann's symbolism was that instead of suggesting to other people how to do things better, workers should go ahead and make things better themselves.

No question, banning the suggestion box is symbolism of the first order. But the very nature of this symbolic act makes it tough to introduce at your own company, unless you are the boss like Marvin Mann. Otherwise, if you do suggest it, your boss could get mad and respond with a symbolic act of his or her own—like suggesting that you take off your wristwatch.

CORPORATE POLICY

APOLOGIES

No one likes to apologize, especially big business. But even corporations make mistakes, so when they apologize, they tend to follow one of several standard formats.

First, there's the attack apology. This has been perfected by ad agencies when people complain about their commercials. For example, the cafeteria workers union complained after a fast-food commercial showed grim scenes at a high school cafeteria. In the attack apology, you say, "Our ad was intended to be humorous and playful, and if somebody somewhere somehow possibly conceivably inadvertently took offense—well, we're sorry." The attack apology, if pulled off right, can make the people to whom you are apologizing seem like nincompoops.

Then, there's the "I did it for your own good" apology, in which you admit wrong but claim a noble purpose. For example, the senior partner at a big Chicago law firm was reprimanded after making racist and sexist remarks while interviewing a job applicant. In his apology, the lawyer said, yes, he made the remarks, but also said he was merely subjecting the woman to a "stress interview" to see how well she could handle intense pressure on the job. He certainly didn't mean any harm. Now, a requirement in this kind of apology is that you can make it while keeping a straight face.

Finally, there's the "wave the flag" apology. You get this after you write a letter complaining about a mysterious inedible object in your box of Crispie Crunchies. Company representatives write back saying how shocked they are. They then go on for five paragraphs describing their stringent quality controls, their pride in the fabulous worldwide reputation of Crispie Crunchies, and how confident they are that Crispie Crunchies will lead them boldly into the next century. Then, they say they're sorry and toss in a one-dollar coupon for your next box of Crispie Crunchies.

Now, you might say that I'm being a bit cynical in these descriptions—that there's a certain lack of sincerity in these apologies, and that they show how clumsy corporations can be. Well, if this is how you feel, all I can say is—that I'm really, really sorry.

TWO-WEEKS' NOTICE

Every working day in America, thousands of people find themselves in an awkward situation known as Two-Weeks' Notice. They've announced to the boss that they've decided to quit and take another job, but will stay on for another two weeks.

Two-weeks' notice is one of those mysterious customs that just seems to have invented itself. Where did it come from? Why is it exactly two weeks, and not one week, or eight days? It's an arbitrary amount of time, yet two-weeks' notice is so deeply ingrained in business etiquette that giving anything less is considered a cold-blooded, flagrant insult to your company.

Once you've given notice, peculiar things start to happen. First is that you never realized how popular you were with your coworkers. People you barely know stop you in the hallway to say congratulations and announce how much they'll miss you. Business cards get slipped in your pocket, with requests that you remember them at your new company. Everyone, including your boss, will loudly proclaim how wonderful you are, using phrases you haven't seen since people signed your high school yearbook. You'll get treated to lunch, drinks, or dinner every day for ten days.

Next, you'll start working harder than you ever had. Now, you'd think that if there was ever a time to kick back, put your feet up on the desk, and goof off, this would be it. After all, you're not worried about getting fired. But some inner compulsion makes you want to leave as a hero, without a single scrap of unfinished business on your desk, so you go into overdrive and work your tail off for two solid weeks.

Finally, the end arrives. You've eaten too much rich food, downed too many drinks, exchanged too many promises to stay in touch with people you really don't want to see again, and worked yourself into a frazzle. Just the right way to embark on a new career track. After two weeks like this an odd thought will probably enter your mind: if you'd known that taking a new job would be such a hassle, you just might have kept the old one.

PHILOSOPHICAL
DIFFERENCES

E arlier this year, a big computer company announced that its number two executive was leaving. The company gave this explanation: the executive and his boss, the CEO, had "philosophical differences."

This odd phrase keeps popping up in corporate press releases when somebody high up is asked to take a hike. In fact, "philosophical differences" ranks right up there with the two other explanation biggies: "Leaving to pursue other business opportunities" and the wonderfully vague "leaving for personal reasons."

Of these three, however, "philosophical differences" is the most puzzling. In all the business meetings I've attended, I've never once heard executives get into an argument over, say, the true meaning of Radical Empiricism. When I attend company training seminars, I don't hear much discussion of the transcendental arguments of Aristotle, or the writings of William James, or the concepts of logical relation theory. In fact, in the business world I don't hear much mention of philosophy or philosophers at all, unless you consider Don Shula a philosopher. But I must be missing something because, otherwise, how could differences in philosophy cause the ouster of so many big-time executives?

Companies should do a better job of avoiding these nasty philosophical clashes. For example, job listings could say things like, "Fortune 500 corporation seeking experienced financial manager who shares chairman's devotion to Spinoza, who can express himself in modal syllogisms, and who can quote from *Being and Nothingness*." And instead of recruiting so many MBAs who know their way around a balance sheet, maybe companies should hire more philosophy majors who know their way around the principles of cosmic consciousness.

Of course, the only sure way to avoid getting into trouble is to not have *any* philosophy, at least until you can figure out what your boss believes. Otherwise, you run the risk of taking a philosophical position that will put you on a high moral ground *and* on a long unemployment line. Remember the immortal words of Descartes, the seventeenth-century philosopher who said, more or less, "I think, therefore I am . . . fired."

THE STRANGE CASE
OF FM2030

W̶hen corporations want to seem enlightened they have a favorite saying—"We treat you like a name, not a number." But now there's evidence that this trend is reversing itself and the *really* enlightened company should treat you like a number, not a name.

This revolution is signaled in *Benchmark* magazine, published by Xerox Corporation. Now Xerox is a pretty straight-laced, button-down corporation. But in a recent issue of *Benchmark* there's an article whose author's name is FM2030. That's right, FM2030. Describing his unusual name, the author, whom I'll call Mr. 30, says this: "Conventional names define a person's past: ancestry, ethnicity, nationality, religion. I'd rather be defined by my future. The name 2030 reflects my conviction that the years leading up to 2030 will be a magical time."

Now I don't know why the year 2030 in particular will be magical, as opposed to 2029. Perhaps this is explained in the author's book, entitled *Are You a Transhuman?*, which I haven't read. But if you think about it, Mr. 30 has a point.

When you hear someone's name in a company, you immediately create a mental image of the person's ethnic group, age, birthplace, and even, God forbid, gender. This is clearly not acceptable in this age when we strive to eliminate all discrimination, real or imagined. Or, if your name is Bob and you are attempting to join a department where there are already five Bobs, you will suffer from traumatic loss of identity. Better that you should have a number that is yours and yours alone.

I've been inspired by the bold words of FM2030. I've decided to shed my given name and define myself by a pivotal event in my life—that far-off day when the mortgage on my house will be paid off. Now that's a vision of the future which I find *really* exciting. In the meantime, just call me DG2021.

THE COMPANY PICNIC

The *Wall Street Journal* reported that more company picnics are getting scheduled this summer,* after a lapse of several years. Three out of four companies are having a summer shindig because management believes they're good for employee morale.

Where they get this idea is a mystery. The company picnic is second only to the office Christmas party in its potential for humiliation and disaster.

Unlike the Christmas party, the company picnic lets you see how your coworkers look in shorts and bathing suits. This alone should make you glad that the picnic happens only once a year. Also, the people who plan these things always select a remote site on the edge of a cliff in the next state, so you waste the weekend trying to find the place and get home.

Then, there's the employee softball game. Beware.

* Broadcast on September 4, 1989.

Some 200-pound ex-jock is going to get overzealous and collide at home plate with a five-foot-tall lady from the personnel department. This will create enough bad feelings to last the rest of the year. On the volleyball court, meanwhile, twenty years of hard work will vanish after you smash a beautiful spike—into your boss's face.

The company president always ends up at the barbecue grill, flipping burgers and looking very uncomfortable. Company presidents get possessed by this compulsive need to cook hamburgers at employee picnics. Are they taught this at Harvard Business School? Are corporations putting strategic charcoal management into executive contracts?

For that matter, is there anyone out there who actually enjoys these picnics? Here's a suggestion: give all employees a little box with hot dogs, soda pop, and marshmallows, and instructions to eat the food on a designated weekend in the privacy and safety of their homes. This may sound like a radical solution, but just think—your company could be losing its best workers to those 25 percent of corporations who offer their employees a great fringe benefit—absolutely *no* company picnic.

WELCOME TO
BOYCOTT CITY*

Every week some group announces a new boycott against a product or corporation. Farmers are boycotting seed company Pioneer Hi-Breed International because the company donates to Planned Parenthood. Environmental groups are boycotting certain brands of tuna fish and disposable diapers. A group of minority publishers is threatening to boycott Procter & Gamble because P&G doesn't advertise enough in their newspapers. A religious group is boycotting Levi Strauss because Levi's is boycotting the Boy Scouts, who in turn are boycotting gays who want to become Scoutmasters.

Now it seems to me that the boycott boom presents a tremendous retailing opportunity. I want to start a warehouse-style store called Boycott City. Inventory would consist entirely of products being boycotted by a legitimate protest organization, which I define as two or more

---

* Broadcast on September 24, 1992.

people with a combined IQ of 14. Manufacturers, grateful to have an outlet for their embattled products, would sell us their goods at deep discounts. Shoppers would buy a Boycott City membership card and then roam the aisles in search of bargains in tuna fish, grapes, seeds, shampoo, 501 jeans, Japanese cars—all kinds of great deals.

I know Boycott City might annoy the groups conducting the boycotts. But I've thought about them, too. You know how Home Depot has free do-it-yourself clinics on weekends? Well, Boycott City would give every group an hour for free demonstrations to explain why the group is boycotting a particular product. Shoppers would fall into three categories: those who agree with the boycott, those who disagree with the boycott, and those who don't give a hoot about the boycott but want to save money. It's a classic win-win-win situation.

So hurry, hurry, hurry on down to Boycott City, where the picket lines meet the checkout lines . . . and where the markdowns will keep you marching back.

OFF-SITE MEETING

The autumn season is when many companies have a big event known as an off-site meeting. This usually takes place at a country resort or some remote site that is supposed to be inspiring. Attendance is "voluntary," meaning that unless you are off closing a megabucks deal with a customer, you better be there.

Now, if you don't know much about an off-site, here are a few pointers.

First, the big word for the weekend is "productive." There will be productive workshops, productive cocktail hours, productive spouse activities. Everyone is so intent on being productive that you'll wonder why the real office doesn't produce this well.

Second, your boss takes the off-site very seriously because it is the one time of the year that the company officially worries about your psyche, ego, and overall spiritual condition. Have enough to eat? Is your room comfortable? Did you find the hiking trail? The company is so darn concerned about you at the off-site that, wonder of wonders, they may hire a facilitator, whose job it is to make sure that everyone is facilitating properly. So, try to assure your boss that you are both happy and facilitated to the max.

Next, decide in advance which sports activity you will pursue. Obviously you don't want to look foolish, but neither do you want to look too good. Demolishing your coworkers on the tennis court with your killer forehand is not likely to breed goodwill around the office. Better you should choose a sport where you can compete at a level of amiable mediocrity.

Now if you still don't really like the off-site, or if the whole experience reminds you, say, of getting root canal work, don't think you are weird. *No one* likes being cooped up off in the woods for the weekend with the same folks you have to see every workday. At least one happy thought can sustain you through the ordeal: on Monday morning things will go back to normal, to *everyone's* immense relief.

IN SEARCH OF
THE CONFERENCE ROOM

I f you work at a big company, you've probably had this experience: You see people wandering the hallway with notebooks and overhead slides. They look confused and anxious. One of them says to you: "Hey, do you know where the conference room is?"

Yes, American business executives have a terrible problem finding their way to conference rooms. Why is this? Well, it starts with what to call a conference room. They often don't have numbers but go by letters, like Conference Room D—not too useful in helping you find them.

When they do have numbers, the numbers often don't correspond to the surrounding offices. And when the numbers do correspond, the conference room is tucked away in its own little corner so you *still* don't know where it is. So off you go, wandering, clutching your overhead slides, and feeling foolish.

The name issue is at the heart of the problem. There are unhelpful names based on relative size, like "The

Large Conference Room" and "The Small Conference Room." Out here in Silicon Valley, companies get creative. There are conference rooms named after Broadway musicals, famous scientists, Star Trek characters, children's movies, and wives of U.S. presidents. This means that you can actually get notified that a meeting has been moved from the Wizard of Oz Room to the Dolly Madison Room. You are still confused about where the Dolly Madison conference room is, but when you see the Martha Washington Room, you can at least assume that you're in the right century.

Your coworkers, meanwhile, are incapable of explaining where the conference room is. They say things like, "Oh, that's the one over by Susan's office" or "That's the one next to Fred's cubicle." Which is fine if you know Susan or Fred, or even if you *are* Susan or Fred. But if you are from another site or a visitor—well, you might want to book your next meeting at, oh, the local Pizza Hut. It may not be much on atmosphere, but at least the odds are better that everyone will find it on time.

LIFE ON
THE ROAD

_____

AIRBORNE GUILT

just got back from a business flight and I'm in a terrible mood. No, it wasn't the food, delays, or even jet lag. My problem is that I'm suffering from Airborne Guilt Syndrome.

I got this condition during the flight when I looked around and saw a planeload of men and women in business clothes, all working furiously. It looked like high school study hall, except everybody was a student council president and everybody was really studying. Everybody, that is, except me.

Now, I'd had several good days on the road, so I packed a sports magazine for a relaxing trip home. BIG MISTAKE. Nobody else was relaxing. They were all *working*. The woman next to me had completely covered her tray table with flow diagrams and blueprints. She had one of those high-tech calculators with two thousand function keys. She had so much gear that I could have rented her space on my tray table, but I was too intimidated to speak.

The two men seated in front of me were having a con-ference with the man sitting in front of them, who had to keep craning his head around to participate. All three were tapping away on laptop computers. They were seri-ous and intense and seemed annoyed when the flight atten-dant interrupted to offer a bag of honey-coated peanuts.

In back of me, a man was shouting into one of those in-flight telephones. He was closing a humongous deal and was pretty excited. I heard words like "reverse leverage" and "mezzanine debt." I wasn't eavesdropping, but it's tough to avoid hearing someone who is shouting about eight inches from your ear.

I fished around in my briefcase for something to work on—anything. Unfortunately, my own work suddenly looked pale and limp when compared with all of these big deals and important decisions that consumed everyone else on the plane. Now I didn't just feel guilty. I felt, well, insignificant.

So what should have been a pleasant return home became a three-hour nonstop exercise in humiliation. However, I am consoled by this thought: if I am such a peon and those other passengers are such big shots, how come they weren't flying first class, but were sitting in coach with me?

BUSINESS HOTELS

Have you heard the latest news from the hotel industry? It seems that every major hotel chain is fighting to win over the business traveler. Hotels are converting their rooms into high-tech business centers, since that supposedly is what business travelers want. The control panel on the TV is now an electronic mail message center. Personal computers, faxes, and photocopiers are becoming standard, as are stenographers and business card print shops.

One hotel has put pads and pencils in its sauna, just in case you want to do a deal while sitting naked and sweating. An executive of one hotel chain says proudly, "We've turned the hotel room into an office away from home."

Well, maybe this is good news if your name is Donald Trump or Rupert Murdoch, but to many of us business travelers, this invasion into the hotel room sounds awful. Let's face it, most business trips aren't glamorous or exciting. They're drudgery and grind. When I'm traveling, what I want from my hotel room is a few hours of privacy and quiet, an edible room service dinner, a hot bath, and a firm mattress. The last thing I want is an extension of the office into my hotel room. Look, if I wanted to work that badly around the clock, it would be cheaper to just put a sleeping bag and an alarm clock into whatever office I'm visiting and skip the hotel altogether.

A good hotel is supposed to be a kind of oasis for the weary traveler, a cease-fire zone after a nonstop day of airport connections, cab rides, and stuffy meetings. But now, your room is considered fair game for anybody in any time zone who wants you to do something. And if you should venture into the sauna for a bit of relaxation, you may be surrounded by three heavily perspiring corporate attorneys wielding pads and pencils! Even Dante couldn't have imagined such torture in his Inferno.

Now, if a hotel really wants to please the business traveler, there are lots of little things it can do. For example, those little freebie containers of shampoo that you find in hotel bathrooms—they're too small. If I have to take a second shower before the maid restocks the bathroom, I run out of shampoo. Forget high-tech electronics. The hotel that can boldly move ahead and put larger samples of shampoo in the bathroom will rate four stars in this business traveler's book.

CORPORATIONS
THAT DISAPPEAR

I have some shocking news about American corporations: they're disappearing.

Now, this has nothing to do with foreign buyers or big
mergers. I mean that American corporations are literally
disappearing—you can't find them on a map. If you don't
believe this, wait until you have to keep an appointment
at a company you've never visited before.

It used to be that you'd simply look at a company's let-
terhead and know it was at 5 Main Street. But nowadays
a company is likely to be in a gigantic development with a
name like Global Finance Tower or World Moolah Center or
Something-Something Square. It doesn't have a street address, or if it does, the address is misleading. For example,
several big companies in Manhattan have headquarters at
Park Avenue Plaza. That's fine, except Park Avenue Plaza
isn't on Park Avenue, it's about half-a-block away, and
you have to enter on either 52nd or 53rd Street.

This can drive you nuts when you are trying to be punctual. In Los Angeles recently, I arrived ten minutes early for an appointment on the 42nd floor of an office complex named after a bank. When I got out of the cab, I discovered that I was in a street-level shopping mall. The guy at the flower stand explained that I had to go through the mall, up an escalator, down a walkway, and around to the elevator. By the time I got to my appointment on the 42nd floor, I was ten minutes late.

Things aren't any better in the suburbs. In Silicon Valley, a company tends to be spread out in one-story, prefab structures that look identical to each other. The location is a remote site that was recently a prune orchard. High-tech businesses like to use catchy, inspirational names for their addresses: Enterprise Way, Opportunity Street, Disk Drive. Nobody in the area, including gas station attendants, knows where the devil these places are.

Whether you're in the city or the suburbs, one thing never changes: You arrive late for your meeting, having shoved the worthless directions you got over the phone way down into your briefcase and frantically making up an excuse about traffic on the freeway. The person you've come to see politely asks, "Have any problem finding the place?" And your response is always the same—you smile, wave your hand, and say, "Oh, *NO* problem, *no* problem at all."

SURVIVING A
TRADE SHOW

Trade show season is in full bloom, with thousands of people descending on places like Orlando, Las Vegas, and Anaheim for these huge events. Convention centers coast to coast are packed with people wearing "Hello, My Name Is" tags.

Now, if you've never attended a trade show, you may feel a bit intimidated about going to one. Well, you'll do just fine if you remember that while walking around the booths and exhibits, you must ask the Three Questions.

1. *What time does the shuttle bus leave?* The primary means of transportation at trade shows is the shuttle bus. It takes you from your hotel to the convention center, from the main hall to the little halls, from the little halls to the spouse activities, and, eventually, back to the airport. If you're out of sync with the shuttle bus schedule, you will have yourself a miserable week.

2. *Do you have dinner reservations?* The really serious schmoozing gets done over dinner. But all forty thousand

persons attending the convention have gotten recommendations for the same six restaurants. Figuring out whom you're having dinner with and then getting into the right restaurant is the most difficult challenge of the trade show.

3. *How do I get all this stuff back into my luggage?* Next to eating, the major activity at a convention is collecting stuff. All kinds of stuff. Buttons, shopping bags, brochures, funny hats, noisemakers, notepads, plus assorted gimmicks and freebies. It would make sense to dump most of it in the wastebasket in your hotel room, but your sense of guilt requires you to wrestle it all into your suitcase.

Once you get home you'll have to field questions from coworkers about what you did in Orlando for three days and four nights. You'll say things about how professionally rewarding the trip was and all the new customers you met. But then you'll get to the nitty-gritty information your listeners really want: "Next time you're in Orlando," you'll say, "you must go to this most sensational little Spanish restaurant I found where the paella is out of this world . . ."

PUTTING YOUR MONEY TO WORK, EVEN IF IT DOESN'T WANT TO

ANNUAL MEETINGS

This is annual meeting season all across Corporate America. It's the one time a year when the people running a public company have to clear their calendar, leave their offices, show up in an auditorium at a specific time, and explain to you and other shareholders what's been going on.

Each year a few annual meetings have verbal fireworks and excitement, but these are rare. Most annual meetings are tidy, dull affairs with about as much drama as a church social. If you're planning to attend your first annual meeting this season, here are some things to watch for.

First, look at the board of directors sitting at the podium next to the CEO. This is your one chance all year to see these directors, most of whom are distinguished and eminent something-or-others who get paid by your company to attend meetings like this. There's likely to be a retired politician, a famous economist, and maybe even a showbiz celebrity who met the CEO at a golf tournament.

Do the board members appear as puzzled by what's going on as you are? Are they gazing blankly into the distance during the auditor's remarks? Do several of them seem to be falling asleep? If so, it may be time to sell your stock and move to another company.

Next, listen to the CEO's speech. Since most companies had a bad year in 1990, how imaginative is he in placing the blame? If he falls back on the obvious excuses—a recession, the Gulf War, economic uncertainty—give him a low grade for creativity. If he comes up with a really unusual excuse—something to do with the rotation of the planets, say, or the aging population of Argentina—he's earned your applause.

Finally, make sure you hang around for the Q&A session. This is the only part of the meeting that is spontaneous. Someone will ask about the treatment of Canadian geese at the pond in front of headquarters. A disgruntled employee will ask embarrassing questions about the high levels of executive compensation. Even a boring annual meeting usually has a couple of chuckles and gasps during the Q&A.

Now, even with these tips in mind, an annual meeting will probably not strike you as razzle-dazzle entertainment. But you might as well try one out because, after all, this is one show that's produced using *your* money.

ANNUAL REPORTS

*i*f you own stock in publicly traded companies, once a year your mailbox gets jammed with annual reports. Most shareholders will do little more than glance at these thick documents. That's too bad because if you only know *where* to look, you can find drama and comedy as good as anything on the best-seller list.

For example, there's the CEO photograph. You might ask, why bother with a photograph? Well, the reason is always the same: we had a photograph last year, and to suddenly leave out the CEO's face would send bad vibes to Wall Street. But how should the boss *look* in the photo? A warm, confident smile? Yes, but if the company lost money or laid off workers, a smile would seem insensitive. A serious, concerned expression? That might imply a lack of optimism about the future. Getting just that right facial expression—not too jovial, not too solemn—can drive people who design annual reports nuts.

Then, there's the problem of which employees to show. Most every company dedicates its report to employees—"our most valuable asset." But which ones get their faces in the annual report? This decision can trigger tidal waves of jealousy, hurt feelings, even guerilla warfare. And don't forget, the persons shown must be balanced to reflect a perfect equality of race, age, gender, national origin, and maybe even height and weight.

Then, there's the listing of major executives in the back of the report. Ever wonder why this list seems as long as the characters in a Russian novel? Well, it's almost impossible to enforce a cutoff on who gets listed and who doesn't. There are powerful people with empty-sounding titles, and there are people with BIG titles—like the presidents of recently acquired divisions—who have no power at all. The only solution is to list everybody, but just use smaller and smaller typefaces.

So try a closer read of your next annual report. Who knows, you might have in your hands the corporate equivalent of a Tom Clancy thriller or a Stephen King horror story. You just have to know where to look.

IPOs

This is a boom year for initial public offerings, or IPOs. An IPO is when a private company sells its stock to the public for the first time. Investors who buy shares of an IPO hope that they've found the next Microsoft, Home Depot, or Amgen before everybody else.

With so many IPOs out there, it's tough to choose which ones to bet on. While I can't tell you which IPO will make you rich, I can suggest which IPOs *not* to invest in.

First, look in the prospectus and count the number of Nobel Prize winners on the board of directors. Then, count the number of university presidents, heads of prestigious foundations, and retired celebrities. Your skepticism should increase in direct proportion to this number. While these intellectual stars may impress you, they probably don't know much about running a small company. They're trading the PR value of their names for shares of stock.

Next, see where the company headquarters is located and calculate its proximity to world-class beaches, glamorous addresses, ski resorts, fine restaurants, and great theatre. Again, your skepticism should rise accordingly. The CEO has located the company based on his lifestyle, not on keeping costs low or staying close to customers. Remember, Bill Gates and Paul Allen started Microsoft from a seedy motel room in Albuquerque, not because they liked seedy motels or New Mexico, but so that they could be close to one of the first personal computer companies.

Third, if you read an article in which a securities analyst raves about the company, check to see if the analyst's firm is also underwriting the offering. Investment banks and brokers are supposed to stay impartial, but they can get, well, casual about IPOs in which they have a financial stake when they are talking to the business press.

Now, you may still decide to invest because of a hunch that the company's plutonium-powered microwidget is a sure thing. Maybe it is. But keep in mind that the insiders who get rich from an IPO do so with OPM—Other People's Money.

WHY NOT BUY
THE WHOLE USA?*

Ross Perot is not someone who likes to kiss babies, eat blintzes, or wear funny hats. That might be why he left the presidential race: as a businessman, the campaigning itself was unappealing. However, Mr. Perot could call the shots in this country without going through the hassle and heartburn of an election. I'm not in the habit of giving free advice to billionaires. But here's my idea for Mr. Perot: instead of running for President, why not just acquire America and take the nation private in a leveraged buyout?

An LBO would be cheaper than an election, and a lot less annoying. With his own funds, plus what he'd get from investors, Perot could buy the fifty states, Guam, Puerto Rico, and the Virgin Islands, and run them as a private enterprise. Real estate prices are depressed and thousands of office buildings are vacant, so the price tag wouldn't even be that steep.

* Broadcast on August 26, 1992.

After the LBO, the new owners of USA Inc. could sell off parts that don't fit with the rest to pay down debt—New York City, for example, or Geraldo Rivera. Instead of having to compromise with Congress, Perot wouldn't *need* Congress, so we'd fire all the senators and representatives. Good riddance.

It's customary after an LBO to clean house, so George Bush would get a generous severance package, an out-placement adviser, use of a secretary, and a ride back to Kennebunkport. There's something in this for Bill Clinton, too. He's a Yale Law School graduate, so he'll be a legal consultant to the LBO.

Instead of President, Mr. Perot would be CEO. Instead of voters, we'd all be shareholders in a privately held corporation. Instead of primaries, conventions, and elections, which are too expensive, we'd just have a national annual meeting, carried live over C-SPAN and hosted by Larry King. We'd outsource the military, perhaps by finding whatever is left of the former Soviet Union's army, navy, and air force and signing them to a five-year contract.

The LBO has other advantages for Mr. Perot. If he got bored with being President, he'd have to resign. However, if he led an LBO and wanted to get out, he'd simply take the country public again, make a tidy profit, and move on.

So how about it, Mr. Perot? You don't have to throw your hat in the ring—just your wallet.

FIRST-TIME HOME
BUYERS, BEWARE

f you are a first-time home buyer, a lot of people are waiting for you to *do* something. Everyone from Alan Greenspan to your local drain-and-gutter man wants you to take advantage of low interest rates, buy that first home, and put the economy back on track.

Of course, you don't really buy a house the first time, you buy a mortgage. And cutting through the dense, often confusing jargon about mortgages can be the worst part of home buying.

For example, when you look for a loan you have to ask about "points." Now, talking about money and points sounds like something a Las Vegas sports gambler should do—"I'll take the Washington Redskins and 6 ½ points." Turns out that points are a percentage the bank charges you for the distinct honor and privilege of lending you the money to buy your house.

There are the two basic types of mortgage: fixed and adjustable. "Fixed" is what pet owners do to animals so they don't have puppies or kittens, so that doesn't sound very good. "Adjustable" means that the bank that charged you the points also reserves the right to adjust downward whatever remains in your checking account at regular intervals of their choosing.

Adjustable loans are tied to a mysterious index, like the cost of funds in your federal district, or Treasury bills, or six-month CDs, or the number of times Lenny Dykstra got hit by a pitch during 1993. The index is published in the newspaper in tiny, tiny print that is almost impossible to read. This is done on purpose because the bank reserves the right to tell you that you were looking at the *wrong* index whenever you think they adjusted your loan incorrectly.

You will also pay a lot of money in "closing costs." These are to compensate the bank for the many valuable services it provides you, such as unstapling and restapling your loan application, sending your application around to different departments until it gets lost, obtaining smudgy copies of your mistake-filled credit report, and having a carefully trained appraiser drive down the street past the house you want to buy. The appraiser takes this little drive to make sure that your house is up to code, which at least sounds like what it is—a code that no one can understand.

After struggling with all of these bizarre concepts you may decide that renting isn't so bad after all and the heck with buying a house. Ah, but then you'll have to contend with a very angry and disappointed Alan Greenspan, not to mention the drain-and-gutter man. In these recessionary times, buying a house isn't your choice—it's your patriotic duty.

SHORT SELLING

---

it takes rare talent to find a crummy company that the rest of the market thinks is hot stuff. That's known as "short selling"—making money when the stock of a company goes not up, but down.

It works like this: You borrow shares from a broker at a high price and sell them for cash. You must return the shares later by buying them back at what you hope will be a much lower price. The difference between the high and the low is your profit.

Many corporate executives look upon short sellers as shady characters who want stock prices to collapse. But short trading is a perfectly legal way to invest. In fact, short sellers are a valuable part of the checks and balances that make a market work efficiently.

Short sellers call themselves "hype detectives." They look for companies whose stock price has been puffed up by wishful thinking. One short seller told the magazine *Institutional Investor* what he looks for in a stock: "Poor management," he said. "Lousy business fundamentals, no product, uneconomic product, poor finances. You know, just a really bad company."

Short selling isn't for everyone. You must have a keen appreciation for the terrible and the awful. Here's a test to see if you have what it takes:

1. Could you attend your company's annual meeting and be happy to discover that the CEO is a blithering idiot?

2. Could you feel a warm inner glow when you try out your company's new kitchen appliance and it blows up?

3. Could you congratulate yourself if your company's director of sales fell asleep while being interviewed by Louis Rukeyser?

If you answered yes to all three questions, you may have a bright future in short selling. But remember, it's not easy to do good things with bad companies. You might have to forget about stocks that are really lousy and invest in ones that are merely mediocre, like the rest of us do.

TICKY-TACKY HOUSES?

Remember a folk song from the 1960s that made fun of "little boxes on the hillside, all made of ticky tacky?" A lot of us who grew up during the 1960s loved this song. The lyrics said exactly how we felt about the suburban houses we lived in: they were boring and bland and conformist and conventional. We swore that we'd be different from our parents when *we* bought a home.

The ticky-tacky song comes to mind with the news that fewer and fewer Americans can afford to buy a home. A big reason for this decline is the way Baby Boomers think about houses.

Somewhere along the line, houses stopped being merely a place to live and became a personal and political statement. A ticky-tacky house in the suburbs meant you were a ticky-tacky individual. A good place to live was in a farmhouse, or a brownstone in a funky urban neighborhood, or in a classic Victorian. A house like that meant you were a sensitive and correct-thinking human being. A house in the suburbs meant that you probably voted Republican and were no fun at parties.

This attitude has made it harder and much more expensive for builders to build. Back in the 1950s, huge developments went up, like Levittown on the East Coast. Economies of scale made these homes affordable. The backyards were small and the designs wouldn't make the cover of *Architectural Digest,* but they were houses and they were in stable communities and they were within the budgets of average working Americans.

Today it's extremely difficult for a builder to get through all the federal, state, and local laws for permission to build more Levittowns. Just mentioning words like "real estate developer" and "subdivision" can start a fistfight at a town meeting. And if the houses get built, the hidden costs of government regulation drive the prices up beyond the reach of the average family.

Yes, it was fun to sing along with those passionate lyrics about the little boxes on the hillside that all looked the same. But to working American families who can't afford to buy *any* home, those ticky-tacky houses don't look quite so tacky anymore.

HEROES, GURUS
AND OTHERS

SALUTE TO
VINKO BOGATAJ

Somewhere in American business there should be a statue in honor of Vinko Bogataj. You may not recognize Vinko Bogataj's name, but you've probably seen him in action hundreds of times. That's because Vinko is the unlucky skier in the opening for the TV show *Wide World of Sports*. He's the guy who loses control and plunges down a mountain, flipping end over end and crashing through the air, while the announcer talks about "The Agony of Defeat."

Now, that was an awful wipeout, a failure. But Bogataj survived. In fact, he continued his career as a world-class skier on the Yugoslavian national team. When *Wide World of Sports* celebrated its anniversary show, Bogataj was in the audience and received a standing ovation.

The lesson in this is that even the best people are due for a wipeout once in a while. It happens to skiers, it happens to people, sometimes it happens to entire companies, even the excellent ones.

Warren Buffett is one of America's smartest and most successful investors. But even he lost money after making what he calls "the intelligent-but-with-some-chance-of-looking-like-an-idiot decision."

In another instance, the head of Japan's wealthiest company, Nomura Securities, was asked what he considered his company's greatest weakness. "We haven't had a failure," he replied. "To me, that is a weakness. Past success can be as much a trap as a guide. Nomura needs a failure." Without a failure, he said, people in a company fool themselves into thinking that what was successful in the past will make them successful in the future, until it becomes almost impossible for them to change at all.

If you haven't had at least one major failure in your business career, don't worry—your turn might be lurking just ahead. When it does happen, think of Vinko Bogataj. And remember that although he was a worldwide symbol of failure, he got to have the last laugh—and a standing ovation.

THE BIG FOUR

H ere's your problem: You've been asked to speak at your company's management conference. You want to end your speech with a quote that will inspire your audience, impress your boss, and boost your career. What do you do? Who do you quote?

Well, you could spend hours with a thick book of quotations. Not only does this take a lot of time, but you risk quoting a little-known writer or politician. This will confuse your audience and annoy your boss. My advice is to concentrate on quoting one of the Big Four—the four people who are the Mount Rushmore for business speakers. Believe me, the Big Four are absolutely, positively guaranteed to produce a quote that will move your audience to tears, or at least to applause.

The Big Four are Winston Churchill, Vince Lombardi, Abraham Lincoln, and Albert Einstein. When it comes to quotations, these guys are what gamblers call a lock—a bet that cannot lose. They are the business speaker's Dream

Team. Executives quote them all the time, but instead of wearing them out, repetition only creates a demand to quote the Big Four even more.

It's odd that hard-driving executives would be so crazy about the Big Four. None of them had a successful business career, and none of them made buckets of money. Churchill was notorious for plunging into debt, and Lincoln suffered several business failures. Einstein disliked big organizations and worked alone. Lombardi ran a football team in a simpler era when players did what coaches told them to do, without a player's lawyer intervening.

Yet, the Big Four have a mystical hold on the minds of managers. The Big Four are well known; they've all been gone long enough to avoid unpleasant connotations; and each had a knack for saying things—or having things attributed to them—that came out profound, inspiring, amusing, or otherwise quotable.

If you're really trying to end your speech with a flourish, you could go for the Grand Slam: quoting the entire Big Four in a virtuoso sweep of rhetoric. The result may not mean much, but it sure will sound great. So, in conclusion, let me say this: although you can fool some of the people all of the time, and while winning isn't everything but is the only thing, and while we will fight them on the beaches with blood, sweat, and tears, we cannot believe that God would play dice with the universe.

HOW TO BE A
BUSINESS GURU

Recently a business magazine ran a cover story on "The New Gurus"—the consultants who provide expensive advice to big companies.

Now, being a guru is a nice job, and you might be wondering how to get into this line of work. Well, lucky for you, I'm something of a guru about gurus and I can reveal to you the three basics for your ascent into gurudom.

First comes The Vision. This is a great sweeping view of what American business must do to survive. You'll need a catchy name for your Vision: excellence, Theory Z, the transparent corporation, horizontal networked empowerment. Remember, in creating your Vision, hyperbole is a virtue and modesty is a vice. As a guru you must compare business today—terrible, inefficient, inhumane, awful—with how it will be if it follows your Vision: wonderful, profitable, innovative, fantastic.

Next comes The Book. Don't worry too much about what you write in The Book, since few will actually read it. Instead, make sure it weighs a lot and is full of exhibits, diagrams, and flowcharts—all of which are impossibly complicated. The Book should have at least two hundred footnotes. And, most important, in the acknowledgments, you should thank everyone you can think of, especially potential clients.

Finally comes The Speech, which is a spin-off of The Vision and The Book. As a guru, you'll spend a lot of time talking to groups, like the Southeast Regional Housewares Distributors Association. Your Speech must make you seem brilliant yet down-to-earth, profound yet entertaining, universal in scope yet incredibly relevant to the particular condition of housewares distribution in the Southeast Region. Once you get The Speech down, it will provide years of service around the guru circuit.

If you follow these basics, you can be a respected, comfortable, middle-class guru. If you are really diligent, you could rise to the level of Cosmic Grandmaster Guru, like Peter Drucker and Tom Peters. You'll be quoted everywhere. CEOs will fly you around in chartered jets to hear your wisdom. Your words will be hoarded like precious rubies; your books will soar like eagles to the top of bestseller lists. You will be rich and will prosper all your years. That, friends, is My Vision.

RUDOLPH THE RED-NOSED
FAST-TRACKER

Since it was first recorded in the 1930s, "Rudolph the Red-Nosed Reindeer" has been one of the most popular songs of the holiday season. But if you interpret its lyrics from the viewpoint of organizational behavior and corporate politics, the song takes on an altogether different quality.

The story begins with Rudolph working in a low-level job in a big company. His coworkers make fun of him and subject him to harassment because of a physical characteristic. Now you'd think Rudolph would have one heckuva job discrimination suit, but for whatever reason, he decides to suffer in silence.

Then one day the CEO, Santa Claus, shows up with a major crisis. He's got to make a big presentation, either to a major customer like Toys "R" Us or to a nervous group of banks who want to pull the plug on Santa's debt financing. The boss personally asks Rudolph to guide him through. So Rudolph pulls an all-nighter, works like a sled dog, and the presentation is saved. Rudolph is a hero and becomes the CEO's favorite.

Well, guess what happens now? All of Rudolph's coworkers *love* him. Donner and Blitzen send notes on E-mail saying, "Rudy, let's do lunch." The elves ask him to put in a good word on their behalf with Santa. The whole North Pole wants him to sign off on their projects. A few reindeer even get nose implants so that they, too, will glow in the dark.

The song ends with Rudolph riding high in the organization. But what happens next year if Rudolph blows his new assignment? Or if Santa asks another reindeer for help? Or if a bigger company buys out Santa's workshop and decides to get out of the cyclical and labor-intensive toy business? You can bet your bottom mistletoe that poor Rudolph will be back out in the cold again.

So, let's recognize the subtle messages in the lyrics of this well-loved song. In fact, it doesn't seem out of line, even in this time of cheer and goodwill, to offer these words of advice: when you're running with a fast crowd, Rudolph, keep your antlers sharpened.

BREAKING THROUGH
THE AD CLUTTER

I t is estimated that the average American is exposed to seven thousand advertising messages in a single day. Breaking through that clutter is enormously difficult. That's why an event that took place a few weeks ago in Las Vegas was so significant.

A small maker of disk drives arranged to have Las Vegas cab drivers ask their passengers, "Do you know who makes the fastest disk drive?" If an employee of the manufacturer was in the cab when the driver asked the question, the cabbie got paid one hundred dollars. The company says it got a terrific response, with lots of people calling up to ask about the product, or to argue about whether their disk drive really was the fastest.

Now, this marketing strategy launched fascinating new possibilities of unlikely people asking you questions about products when you least expect it.

For example, airline pilots. Imagine yourself somewhere over the Midwest, adjusting your seat back and tray table, when you hear, "This is Captain Baker speaking. We're cruising at thirty-five thousand feet, the Colorado River is on the left, and, by the way, can anybody name the gentle antacid that provides fast, fast relief and which four out of five doctors recommend?"

Or waiters. You're looking over the menu and Bruce, your waiter tonight, asks, "Would you like the soup or the salad? Red wine or white? Italian or Thousand Island? And, say, can you identify the sporty luxury sedan with automatic tilt-down steering and a 278-horsepower V8 engine?"

Or the guy in the tollbooth on the New Jersey Turnpike. You ask him which exit to take to get to South Orange. He asks you if you can name the disposable diaper that keeps baby dry no matter how wet it gets?

Now you can't have the person asking the question actually *knowing* something about the product. There has to be a dazzling degree of the ridiculous in the combination of the person and the product—like cab drivers and disk drives. And who knows? This trend may someday reach the heights of the ridiculous and include an occupation that involves talking to a lot of people, but which doesn't require being especially knowledgeable about anything. Gee, that sounds a lot like a radio commentator.

THE DOCTOR
WILL SELL YOU NOW

Your mood in a doctor's office is controlled by two emotions: anxiety and the desire to get the heck out of there as soon as you can. But in a doctor's waiting room, you are swamped by people trying to sell you something.

I recently accompanied my wife on a routine doctor's appointment. The waiting room was dominated by a blabbering TV set, tuned to a channel specially made for people who are wondering what strange affliction they have. The programs were thinly disguised commercials that pretended to be medical updates.

When I asked the receptionist to turn the TV off or at least turn it down, she claimed she couldn't. The channel was piped in and could not be controlled in the office. We were media hostages! So, like characters from a George Orwell novel, we sat fuming while the TV blathered on.

I tried to distract myself by reading the literature on the coffee table. This also turned out to be disguised advertising, with titles like "Keep Kids Safe This Summer," "How to Make Extra Cash," and "Are You Aging Gracefully?" There was one of my favorite magazines, *Diaper Digest,* which had been provided by Tiny Tots Diaper Service. There were also brochures sponsored by various pharmaceutical companies that posed as learned essays on scary diseases.

Of course, this advertising barrage is justified by the same excuse: "We're educating the public." But that's baloney. I'm visiting a medical office to get educated *by the doctor,* not by the waiting room. If I want to read health brochures, I'll go to the public library and save the expense of an office visit.

If you're offended by these ads, tell your doctor. The law says we have the right to privacy of our medical records. But we also have the right to the privacy of our minds, and that includes not being held as a captive audience to a sales pitch. If doctors insist on converting their offices into advertising salons, they should be required to provide two waiting rooms—one for the companies advertising to the sick, and the other for people who are, well, sick of all the advertising.

THE KARMA
OF CAR MANUALS

just bought my first new car since 1981. Like an automotive Rip Van Winkle, I discovered that a whole lot has changed in the car world. For example, the owner's manual. My old manual was almost unreadable, written by engineers for engineers. My new manual is very sensitive, caring, compassionate—very 1990s.

Why, the very first chapter of the manual is dedicated to—me. These pages candidly explore the deep personal relationship between me and the car company. Here's an example: "Our work must be done with you in mind. We are dedicated to learning what you want.... We must treat one another with trust and respect." The chapter *begs* me to just let them know of my slightest concern. I wasn't sure if I was reading a car manual or one of those "I'm OK, You're OK" books.

Furthermore, my new manual can't do enough to help me, even suggesting how to look something up: "If the word you chose is not listed," it says, "think of other related words and look them up." This was wise counsel. When I looked up "sun roof," the manual gently informed me that it's now called a "moon roof." And what I called a car radio back in the 1980s is now called a high-level electronic audio sound system, with its *own* 43-page operating guide.

But the most fascinating chapter in the new manual is called "Vehicle Sounds" and describes noises my car will make when it isn't feeling well, such as buzz, chatter, chirp, chuckle, and clunk. There's also "growl/howl," which are "low guttural sounds like an angry dog." And my favorite, "roar," whose description sounds absolutely Gothic: "a deep, long, prolonged sound like that made by an animal or wind."

Well, I'm really pleased that my new car manual is so caring and sensitive. But all the same, I hope my new car won't be chuckling, clunking, or growling like an angry dog until at least well past the year 2000. That's when I plan to rise again from Rip Van Winkle mode and buy my *next* new car.

ABOUT THE AUTHOR

David Graulich has been a regular commentator on the public radio program *Marketplace* since 1989. His focus is the business world and its odd, quirky, and offbeat aspects. Most of the commentaries concern the humor hidden within everyday work life. David's friend, San Francisco writer Chris Barnett, says, "Graulich is like Garrison Keillor, except instead of small-town America, David talks about Corporate America."

A native of New Jersey, Graulich is a 1976 graduate of Dartmouth College, where he was managing editor of the campus newspaper and wrote a weekly humor column, "Second Thoughts." He started his career with the *Daily Register,* a small newspaper on the New Jersey shore, and was a staff reporter in the Cleveland bureau of the *Wall Street Journal.* The high point of his *Wall Street Journal* experience was a hard-hitting investigation of the dustpan industry, in which Graulich discovered the two primary reasons that consumers replace old dustpans—(1) people break off the handle after using them as pooper-scoopers or snow cleaners; and (2) they accidentally drive over them in the garage.

When, by some inexplicable oversight, the Pulitzer Prize committee didn't reward Graulich's achievement, he left newspaper work and entered corporate public relations. He was a speechwriter and publicist for Squibb Corporation in Princeton, New Jersey, and then joined McKinsey & Co., the management consulting firm, where he was a public relations manager in New York and San Francisco. At McKinsey, Graulich promoted the best-seller *In Search of Excellence* by Tom Peters and Bob Waterman, and the writings of Japanese business expert Kenichi Ohmae. Both Squibb and McKinsey also proved fertile ground for many of the experiences and observations that would later become *Marketplace* commentaries.

In 1987, while living in San Francisco, Graulich launched his own public relations business. He called it Maxfield Public Relations, taking the name from a favorite artist, American illustrator Maxfield Parrish. Maxfield Public Relations is now based in San Bruno, California, a suburb of San Francisco. The company handles writing assignments and public relations for corporate clients that include PepsiCo, Inc., and CSC Index.

Graulich relaxes by playing the piano and collecting parodies of the World War I recruiting poster, "I Want You" by James Montgomery Flagg. He and his wife,

Rebecca, share their home on the San Francisco Peninsula with Buddy, a 100-pound Bouvier des Flandres dog whom David describes as "a cross between an Irish wolfhound and a small donkey."